FIVE KEYS ON HOW TO HEAR

GOD'S VOICE AND DIALOGUING

WITH GOD

REV EMMANUEL NEBA

ISBN 978-0-9576375-0-4

Printed in Great Britain for

WORLD ON FIRE MISSION PUBLISHING

102 High Street

Uckfield, East Sussex

TN22 1PX

CONTENTS

DEDICATION

This book is dedicated:

* To glory of our Lord Jesus Christ.

* To World on Fire Mission Family and Partners

* To Full Gospel Mission (Cameroon), The Church in Nepal, Arise and Shine for Christ Ministries (USA), UK World Evangelism Churches and Council, Christian Fellowship - Schaafheim (Germany)

* To Christian Leadership University/Seminary (USA)

ENDORSEMENTS

In this book you will learn the Biblical and practical ways in which you can know and experience God more fully.

It is my prayer that as you study the teaching Emmanuel presents and do what he says according to the Scriptures, your life would never remain the same.

My wife and I met Emmanuel at a church in East Sussex when he came to the UK to be joined to his wife Eunice. God joined us together, knitting our lives and experiences in a way possibly we might have naturally not chosen. The Holy Spirit did this, in order that through hearing God's voice each of us would grow as individuals and as collective.

Emmanuel's practical testimonies back up God's authored word, and make for powerful, inspiring and energising reading. As you read, ask the Holy Spirit and Jesus Himself to reveal themselves to you. The word says that we are not just to be hearers of God's word but doers of it **(James 1:22).**

I wholeheartedly recommend this book for anyone who would like to enjoy walking intimately with God by learning to hear His voice.

Bless you.

Mr Chris Gray
Client Director & Consulting,
Oracle Corporation

FOREWORD

HOW I OVERCAME MY STRUGGLE ON LEARNING HOW TO HEAR THE VOICE OF GOD

Hearing the voice of God is one of my foundational values today and it has been for many years. This teaching and experience on How to Hear God's voice and Dialogue with God quickly points out how the Bible is full of visions, dreams and revelations as the Lord was continually speaking to people in the bible. It was clearly the will of the Lord to also speak to me. The fear of being misled is thoroughly addressed pointing out the difference between the 'world of magic and supernatural beliefs and practices,' relating to the occult, new age teachings and Biblical Truth. I really needed to hear and understand clearly this difference from the Lord through his word.

God is a loving, caring, speaking and communicating Father. This hunger and searching brought me into a place of hearing and knowing the heart of my Heavenly Loving Father. My inner being learnt experientially that He is a very personal God, wanting to commune with me and share His heart with me. Hearing His loving confirmation and direction strengthened my relationship and built intimacy with Him. Lasting fruits are growing in my ministry.

I always believed that Christians should be able to hear God's voice. I know He wants to guide us continually and one of the ways He guides us is by His *still small voice* (**1 Kings 19:11-13**). Yet no matter how hard I tried, I never could hear that still small voice speaking to me. But the Lord had seen the desire of my heart to know His voice, a desire that could not be overpowered even by repeated failures and disappointments.

He gradually led me to the right resources to teach me the skills I needed: inner stillness; spontaneity; vision; journaling and waiting. When all these individual parts were in place, I realised that I had received much more than I expected. I was seeking for a still small voice but I found God as a person (**Matthew 7:7-8**). I was seeking for guidance but I found a loving caring Father *who did not spare His own Son but delivered Him up for us all* (**Romans 8:32**). I was seeking for the will of God but I found a relationship with our Lord and Saviour, Jesus Christ (**Psalm 23**).

Since I have been able to discern the voice of the Lord in my heart, I have moved into a life of sweet fellowship with Jesus. I no longer live under law, for now I am governed by love. Rules have given way to a personal relationship. I am in daily contact with my Lord, and my whole life has been changed. My personality, my family, and my ministry have all been altered by the wisdom and compassion of Jesus, who is now available to me. My heart has been convinced that the love

God has completely changed me and I will never be the same again. I began sharing my newly gained knowledge, teaching others how to hear God's voice and to acquire a breakthrough in two-way dialogue with God. Many have joyfully entertained this new found freedom of speaking and listening to God. The church is now beginning to hear God's voice and see God's vision for His people, *to grant to those who mourn in Zion to give them a beautiful headdress instead of ashes, the oil of gladness instead of mourning, the garment of praise instead of a faint spirit; that they may be called oaks of righteousness, the planting of the LORD, that he may be glorified* (**Isaiah 61:3**). The time for mourning has passed. The church is awakening to her sins, her responsibilities and her kingdom authority. The kingdom of this world shall indeed become the Kingdom of our Lord and of His Christ. He will reign through us in every aspect of our lives on this earth.

It is my prayer that the Lord will anoint this teaching and experience, using it to bring people like me into a new dimension of Christianity, a place of two-way dialogue with God, talking with God 'face-to-face as a man talks with his friend,' (**Numbers 12:8**).

Emmanuel Neba

INTRODUCTION

A DIVINE APPOINTMENT

January 1993

Emmanuel! Get Up! Kneel down and look!

This commanding voice woke me from a sound sleep and I knelt down next to my bed. Though I had never heard it before, or since, I immediately knew that I had heard the audible voice of God.

"What? What?" I said in confusion.

"Wake up! I am going to show you a vision!"

"Wow!" I said as I knelt down, "Show me Lord."

That night as I knelt at my bedside, the Holy Spirit gave me the precious gift I had been seeking for so long and launched me into the calling that would become my passion for the rest of my life. Now He brought together all I had learnt after many years of ministry, prayer and hearing God's voice and showed me how it all fitted into five simple keys that were revealed in **Habakkuk 2:1-3.**

HOW I GOT THERE

When I accepted the Lord at the age of fourteen, my immediate hunger was to learn God's word and become a biblical man. After graduating from High School, I became a businessman but without peace in my heart, due to God's call in my life. I started studying the Word with the help of my Pastor and spiritual leaders. I obeyed God's calling by going to towns and villages in my Province to share the good news of the Lord Jesus Christ, rather than going to the University to study mathematics as I had previously planned.

It was no surprise, therefore when I found a passionate desire within me to make the Bible real, practical, and down-to-earth in my life. As I studied and taught the people, I began to see that the voice of God, or the 'Word of the Lord' as the prophets called it, was very real and a continuous theme in scripture. I noticed from Genesis to Revelation, that men and women heard God's voice speaking to them. A hunger grew within me to hear God's voice in my own heart. A strong desire to become a spiritual man and to understand the ways of the Spirit began to burn as I recognized that I could only become a biblical man, if I too, could hear the voice of God.

So I began searching for God's voice within my heart. I wailed expectantly for the inner audible voice of God to speak to me and say, "Hello, Emmanuel, this is God." But nothing happened. I listened and listened, but I could not discern any 'voice of God.' All I heard were thoughts flowing through my mind until I eventually wandered off in pointless daydreams.

It was extremely frustrating! Prayer simply didn't work for me and I failed to see the reason why. I fasted for days and even weeks, I went back to the Scripture to ensure that the people in the Bible truly heard His voice. Yes, God unmistakably confirmed that in every covenant from Genesis to Revelation He had spoken to His people. At that time, God graciously placed in my life a pastor in my local church, who was able to clearly hear the voice of God and speak it in wonderful prophecy. I marvelled at the purity, power and accuracy of the way he spoke the word of the Lord. I decided to ask him what he did to hear the voice of God. He patiently shared his own experience. Finally I realised that He was naturally intuitive, but the fear of being misled kept me from hearing God's voice. He spoke a prophetic word to me about the consequences I would face if I continued to suppress His voice and the calling of God in my life. This actually happened a few years later. I stepped out of faith and started applying the instinctive flow of God by using the five keys of hearing God's voice.

I thank God that even when we are unaware of it, His hand is leading us. Through all my hunger and searching, He was leading me one small step at a time. Most of the steps were not even noticeable at the time, just seemingly insignificant events or 'fortunate' circumstances. Yet today I can look back and see how the hand of God moved in my life. Through all my failures, disappointment and confusion, He was always working all things out for my good (**Romans 8:28**).

CHAPTER 1

INTRODUCING THE FIVE KEYS FOR HEARING GOD'S VOICE

The beginning of the revelation came in a quiet way. I spent much of the following months studying everything I could on 'how to hear God's voice' and dialoguing with God.

I will stand upon my watch…*And will watch to see* what *He will say to me*… *And the Lord*…*said, Write the vision*…. *Though it tarry, Wait for it; because it will surely come,* it *will not tarry.* (**Habakkuk 2:1-3** emphases added)

Obviously Habakkuk could discern the sound of the Lord's voice in his heart. He said, "Then the Lord said." Also throughout his writing, Habakkuk recorded what God had spoken to him. Therefore he knew the sound of God's voice.

The first key of hearing God's voice is found in Habakkuk's phrase, **"I will stand upon my watch,"** to meet with the Lord regularly in a special place of prayer. Habakkuk knew how to go to a quiet place and quieten his own thoughts and emotions, so he could sense the spontaneous flow of God within.

Habakkuk 2:1 says, "*I will stand upon my watch, and set me upon the tower*…." It is wonderful what I learnt from this verse. Habakkuk knew that in order to hear God's quiet, inner, spontaneous thoughts, he had to first go to a quiet place, (probably the walls of Jerusalem) and still and quieten his own thoughts and emotions. Just like the Psalmist who encourages us to be still and know that He is God (**Psalms 46:10**). How wonderful it is to know that there is a deep inner knowing (spontaneous flow) in our spirit that each of us can experience when we quiet our flesh and our minds. Our thoughts, will and emotions take place in the flesh and mind, since our spirit is eternally redeemed (**Hebrews 9:11-12**).

Loving God through a quiet worship song is most effective to still my thoughts and emotions. I learnt to put on His robe of righteousness, seeing myself spotless before the presence of God by thoroughly repenting and receiving the washing of the Blood of the Lamb (**Romans 8:1-2**) and dismissing any accusing thoughts of the devil (**2 Corinthians 10:5-6**)

Illustration:

In 1994, I was going to a farm with my friend Harrison Nde, who was also hungry for the supernatural and hearing God's voice. We were discussing and wondering if God had called us into full-time ministry. God had used us in the area of healing and deliverance but not the raising of the dead, as Jesus commanded us in Matthew 10:8. We then prayed that God would give us a sign.

After a few hours working on the farm we felt very hot so we decided to go swimming in the river beside the farm, the rest of Harrison's family kept on working. Unknown to me, while we were in the river, Harrison suddenly developed a very high fever and a serious migraine. He came out of the river with tremendous pain and migraine. I was not aware of the magnitude of his situation, but when I realised he was not coming back into the river, I went to find him. When I saw him I realised that something was seriously wrong. He told me to pray as we both felt it was a spiritual attack. We were not aware that the river where we were swimming was an evil river and much demonic worship and ritual took place there.

It was taboo in the village to swim in that river and we had just signed our own death certificate. Harrison was in terrible pain and I was praying as hard as I could, but the more I prayed the more the pain increased. Harrison's hand and head went numb; I thought this was beyond me and I needed some people to join me in prayer. So I shouted to the rest of the family who were still working on the land. The sound of my shouting sent many alarm bells to his mother and as she ran to us, she was obviously, deeply worried. Harrison's head, hands and legs were now totally numb.

I kept encouraging Harrison in the word to *have faith in God* (**Mark 11**:22) and to begin to move his body. Suddenly his mother cried out loudly saying, "This is exactly how my father died". When she had given her life to Christ the people in the village warned her that her son would die in the same manner as she had become a Christian and renounced the village tradition. I told her not to believe that, but have faith that her son would not die. Then all of a sudden Harrison faintly spoke the word "faith" three times and then gave up the ghost. The whole place was therefore very quiet and Harrison's mother just wished to die as well. One of Harrison's relatives ran to inform the villagers that Harrison was dead. Suddenly the power of the Holy Spirit fell on me and scriptures like (**Matthew 10:8**), *heals the sick, cleanse the lepers, raise the dead, cast out demons. Freely you have received, freely give* leapt out of my spirit, saying you can raise the dead if you believe, nothing is impossible with God.

A supernatural faith came upon me but I needed to still my own thoughts and emotions, so that I can sense God's flow of thoughts and emotions within me. I started worshipping and praising God in the spirit. The Lord then led me to a particular location by the river where the demonic god of the river resides. Pointing my finger to the exact location in the river, I cursed the habitation of that spirit to die and to bind the spirit into the abyss. As soon as I did that, joy came into my spirit, even though Harrison was lying on the riverbank lifeless. I was led by the Holy Spirit through spontaneous thought to walk towards him and speak saying "Harrison, have life in Jesus' name." I did exactly as the Spirit led me and then I turned away from Harrison, to avoid doubt, faced the river and started singing in the spirit this song:

"You are the Lord, that is Your Name. You will never share Your glory with anyone. You will never share your glory with anybody. Almighty God, that is Your name."
And also, "Thank you Jesus"
An hour passed and suddenly I heard a shout from Harrison's mother saying something like "Harrison, what happened to you?" Then he asked faintly "What are we doing here and why is Emmanuel crying and singing by the bank of the river?" Then I turned around and behold, my friend was back alive!!!

His mother kept asking Harrison what had really happened. He said he was going somewhere and heard people singing and dancing. It was a wonderful scene when suddenly he found himself there. He himself could not explain how he got there. His eyes were changed like those of a baby and while we were walking home we thanked God. The villagers came to take Harrison's corpse home and they actually walked passed us thinking we were ghosts as they believed Harrison was still dead, but his ghost would still be walking around! After some distance, they called to Harrison's mother to enquire if what they saw was real. She responded, "Yes!"

A week later, Harrison's relative, who was the eye witness of the whole incident, came to the farm and saw some young hunters fighting to kill an unusual animal with human features from the same river. This animal spat water at them, which never touched them. They succeeded in killing the animal eventually and brought it to an elder of the village. He was surprised at what they had done and immediately sent them to the palace. The village chief was also very surprised how they could have killed the animal, as it was the river god of the village, and they were fortunate to be alive. The chief then took the animal away. This story was told by Harrison's relative to explain how the killing of this animal was possible because I pronounces a curse of death on the habitation of the river god. Both these incidents led to this woman's salvation, a relative of Harrison.

After this incident, I came to the conclusion that, *for all the promises of God in him are 'yes' and in him 'Amen', unto the glory of God by us* (**2 Corinthians 1:20**). Harrison and I were now fired up for any work for God and we believed that, *the things which are impossible with men are possible with God* (**Luke 18:27**). So I learnt always to still my own thoughts and emotions, so that I can sense God's flow of thoughts and emotions within me.

The second key is found in Habakkuk's phrase, "*I will watch to see.*" I asked myself why he said it that way. Why didn't he say, 'I will listen to hear what he will speak to me?' It makes more sense to me that one would listen to hear spoken words than watch to see them. By the time this question was answered in my heart and mind, God had opened up an entirely new revelation concerning the place of dreams and visions in prayer. I had never considered opening the eyes of my heart to God and looking to see what He wanted to show me. This was wonderful, exciting and amazing. You must look for God to speak to you in dreams and visions! There are four types of visions and dreams: inner vision (**2 Kings 6:5-7**), outer vision (**Joshua 5:13**), trance (**Acts 10:10-16**), and vision of the night (**Acts 16:9**). The Bible showed that the presence or the absence of vision will determine whether or not people become lazy, or worse, '*cast off restraint,*' oblivious to the law (**1 Samuel 3:1**; **Proverbs 29:18**). The presence of vision creates hope and brings change when articulated with enthusiasm (**Luke 24:23**).

What I learnt here was very interesting. Habakkuk said, "*I will keep my watch to see*" and God said, "*Write the vision.*" This is something not usual in our days which is governed by common sense or logic, and intellectual and analytical thought. By opening the eyes of our heart and looking into the spirit world we see what God wants to show us and recording it.

This is really an intriguing idea. Now I'm making use of what God gave me (eyes of my heart) to see in the spirit world the vision and movement of Almighty God. The spirit world is very real, full of angels, demons, the Holy Spirit, the Omnipresent

God and His Omnipresent Son Jesus. It is clearly seen in the Bible from Genesis to Revelation. Paul said in **Ephesians 1:18-23**, *I pray also that the eyes of your heart may be enlightened in order that you may know the hope to which He has called you, the riches of His glorious inheritance in the saints, and His incomparably great power for us who believe. That power is like the working of His mighty strength, which He exerted in Christ when He raised Him from dead and seated Him at his right hand in the heavenly realms, far above all rule and authority, power and dominion and every title that can be given not only in the present age but also in the one to come and God placed all things under His feet and appointed Him to be head over everything for the church, which is His body the fullness of Him who fills everything in every way.* How I wish that the church today could grasp this important truth!

Illustration:

During my quiet time, I always fix the eyes of my heart upon Jesus being present with me and I watch him speak to me, although I do not physically see Him, I could feel Him. But after learning that I could watch Jesus as He speaks to me, doing and saying the things that are on His heart, I can now see Him with the eyes of my heart. Our *Immanuel, which is translated, 'God with us'* (**Matthew 1:2-3**). I got up at 3am in the morning, looking and looking with the eyes of my heart fixed upon Jesus. How amazing it was when I saw Him, it was like the brightness of beams of sunlight! I knew immediately it was Jesus because I became unworthy, empty and in awe of His presence and He spoke with a gentle voice, "look at the stars above, see what I want to show you," I looked and could not see the stars at first because the sky was bright. Then all of the sudden darkness came upon the sky and I started to see the stars when the sky was at its darkest. It was amazing to see the beauty of the morning stars, shining and very bright. I realised that this inner vision was spontaneous and in a manner similar to receiving a flow of spontaneous inner thoughts. How easily it came. Jesus looked at me with compassion at that moment and then in a loving manner He said, "the problems and difficulties you are facing are like that dark sky but the darker it becomes, the more you will shine like the morning stars. All that you need during that darkness is to stay focussed with your eyes fixed on Me, and then every problem or suffering will be your promotion". **Isaiah 45:2-3**, *I will go before you and will level the mountains; I will break down the gates of bronze and cut through bars of iron.*

I will give you the treasures of darkness, riches stored in secret places, so that you may know that I am the Lord, the God of Israel, who summons you by name. Thank God for **key #2**, now I have no limitation or hindrance in using the eyes of my heart and it has brought more life and excitement in my quiet time.

The third key is found in Habakkuk's phrase, "*He will say to me,*" to listen for the word of God. Hearing God's voice is learning what His voice spoken within us would sound like.

Rather than being an inner audible voice, I discovered that God's voice in our hearts generally sounds like a flow of spontaneous thoughts. Yes, God graciously spoke to me in an audible voice that night and on four other occasions, but that is certainly not the norm. In fact, it is more likely an indication that I was too stubborn or thick-skinned to get His message in any other way! Like Paul on the road to Damascus, I had to be "hit over the head" in order to hear what He had to say to me.

The Lord will take drastic measures if necessary, but He would rather we learnt to discern Him speaking through spontaneous thoughts from within our hearts.

Illustration:

I remember what happened to me on the 17th September 2005 in Nepal, when I was invited to a healing crusade by an underground church in a town called Nijgadh. The church told me it was impossible to hold an open-air crusade in that town. Their reasons were that the village was a stronghold of witches and wizards, many of which were held in captivity and bondage. Knowing that Christianity was banned in Nepal at that time, I heard a quiet voice in my heart like a flow of spontaneous thought saying, "do not be afraid, go for the first open-air healing crusade in the history of the town of Nijgadh.

Keep on speaking and do not be silent, for I am with you and no one is going to attack or harm you, because I have many people in this city" (**Acts 18:9-10**). I accepted the invitation and went to the crusade. As I was walking to the pulpit to take the microphone another spontaneous thought came to me in the form of a word of knowledge. "There is someone here among the crowd suffering from a tumour on the brain, unable to walk and very popular in this town". After receiving this word of knowledge, the Lord asked me through spontaneous thought to openly challenge the witches and wizards in that town, by asking the person to whom the word of knowledge was aimed at to stand up before the crowd of more than a thousand people. When they brought him, it was exactly as I heard from the spontaneous thought. I challenged them to use their witchcraft power or the powers of their many gods to heal the man with a physical sign of getting up by himself from the wheelchair to walk and dance. Then everyone present would believe in their gods and their powers. But if not, I would openly challenge them in the name of Jesus, by declaring to them that, "before the end of this service, this man will be healed and will rise up, walk and dance before them, so that they will fear the Lord Jesus Christ and know that He alone is the true God". It was difficult for me to openly declare that statement because the people were mostly Hindus, Muslims or Buddhists, with little or no knowledge of our Lord Jesus Christ. But I obeyed the voice of God that came to me through a flow of spontaneous thoughts and did what He said. I was very excited and happy when this man stood up and began to walk and dance before the end of the service with his hands in the air saying in Nepali language, "the Lord has healed me." So we rejoiced together with the crowd before our Lord Jesus Christ for His faithfulness, in the same manner as King David and the people of Israel did when the Ark of God was brought back to the City of David (**2 Samuel 6:14-16**). It is wonderful to know this truth, "God's voice in our heart is like a flow of spontaneous thoughts." All we need to do is to be tuned to this spontaneity. As a result, many Hindus, Muslims and Buddhist received the Lord Jesus Christ as their Lord and personal Saviour, which brought great revival in the town. That town would never be same again.

The fourth key is demonstrated in **Habakkuk 2:2**, when the Lord said, *"Write the vision,"* to keep a journal of things that God says. What an incredible idea, actually writing down my dialogue with God! And yet I soon saw that the whole book of Habakkuk is the story of a man who wrote down his prayers and the answers that he received in response from God. And it was God who commanded him to write it down. This process is called 'journaling.' Many examples of this are found in the book of Psalms, the Prophets and the entire book of Revelation. It always surprises me to find the church spending so much time discussing doctrines based on just a few verses of scripture, only to neglect a doctrine that is commanded and demonstrated in several hundred verses of Scripture. It makes me believe the church today is sleeping and lifeless and needs an infusion of the Holy Spirit.

What I learnt from my journaling was there was no need to test it while it was being received, which would stop the flow of God's inner spontaneous thoughts, because I would always have the opportunity later to test and examine it carefully, making sure that it lined up with Scripture. Before the idea of journaling, I was testing it while receiving and asking many questions in my mind whether it was from God, the devil or my own thoughts, which always hindered the flow and kept me away from journaling.

Illustration:

In 2003 there was a time in my life, where it seemed like the whole kingdom of darkness had risen up against me and God was like a million miles away from me. So I spent time alone with God in a very dry and lifeless moment in my spiritual life. I started asking God some questions and writing down His response. Below is what I wrote down in my journaling book.

Are you still there God?

God did not answer as I expected to hear an audible voice. Instead it was a flow of spontaneous thoughts saying, "Almost all children of God experience periods where their quiet times are dry, lifeless and God appears to be far away. It can continue even after they have confessed every known sin and exercise every possible spiritual discipline, as you have done".

So what should I do when you are silent for no apparent reason?

Then the Lord answered, "Don't panic just stay where you are. There are seasons of spiritual growth in which I choose to withdraw the sense of My presence for a time, so that your trust and faith in Me will develop to a higher level. If you remain faithful in your quiet times during seasons of silence, you will be able to powerfully demonstrate a commitment to Me that is unconditional, without expectation. You are seeking to give to Me, regardless of the spiritual return. As surely as the sun rises, I will eventually speak and will summon you by name."

Finally, what will become of me when this season is over?

The Lord answered, "When you leave the darkness, you will realise you have grown spiritually. Like precious diamonds, new riches of faith will be developed in your dark places. It will open and expose your character and weaknesses that have remained hidden until now, removing the obstacles that have kept you from experiencing abundant life. It can change you from unrefined ore into a vessel of pure gold.

Job 23: 8-14, *"Behold, I go forward, but he is not there, and backward, but I do not perceive him; on the left hand when he is working, I do not behold him; he turns to the right hand, but I do not see him. But he knows the way that I take; when he has tried me, I shall come out as gold. My foot has held fast to his steps; I have kept his way and have not turned aside. I have not departed from the commandment of his lips; I have treasured the words of his mouth more than my portion of food. But he is unchangeable, and who can turn him back? What he desires, that he does. For he will complete what he appoints for me, and many such things are in his mind".*

Since I started journaling I realised the truth of His word and why the prophet Amos said, *surely the Sovereign Lord does nothing without revealing His plan to His servants the prophets* (**Amos 3:7**). I found that I was actually dialoguing with God after going back to my journal. It is always amazing and one of my most exciting moments when I look back in my journal. Whenever I'm facing situations which need counseling, I discovered that my best counsel was what I had written down during my quiet time. Now I'm teaching many local churches and missions about hearing God's voice with confidence and boldness.

Finally, the **Fifth Key** is demonstrated in Habakkuk 2:3, **_"Wait for it; because it will surely come,"_** to wait for God to bring it to pass, '_it will surely come.'_ This is the most difficult key to understand because human nature wants answers either now or wants to know when it will happen if it does not happen now. Waiting is, by its nature, something only the humble can do with grace.

In **Acts 1:1-8**, Jesus was speaking His last words to His disciples before being taken to His throne at the right hand side of the Father. The kingdom of God, the divine rule in human hearts, lives, and situations, was a prominent theme in Jesus' teaching. Jesus began to do and teach the Kingdom through the Spirit's power (**Luke 4:18, 19**), and in Acts He is about to transfer that power and responsibility to His disciples by baptizing them in the same Spirit that had authorised His ministry. In verse 5, Jesus said, _for John truly baptized with water; but ye shall be baptized with the Holy Ghost not many days hence._

Look at the disciples' response in verse 6, _so when they were assembled, they asked Him, Lord, is this the time when You will re-establish the kingdom and restore it to Israel?_

The disciples were still thinking of the messianic kingdom in terms of political powers. Why? They were tired of waiting and being under the government of the Romans. They were looking for physical not spiritual deliverance, but Jesus who 'all knowing' knew their actual need. Learn from Jesus' response in verse 7&8.

He said to them, It is not for you to become acquainted with and know what time brings [the things and events of time and their definite periods] or fixed years and seasons (their critical niche in time), which the Father has appointed (fixed and reserved) by His own choice and authority and personal power. But you shall receive power (ability, efficiency, and might) when the Holy Spirit has come upon you, and you shall be My witnesses in Jerusalem and all Judea and Samaria and to the ends (the very bounds) of the earth.

In His reply Jesus corrected their misconception and adjusted their perspective concerning the kingdom of God and God's timing.

Deuteronomy 29:29 says, *the secret things belong unto the Lord our God, but the things which are revealed belong to us and to our children forever, that we may do all of the words of this law.*

Let us meditate on the following scriptures.

Psalm 37:7

Amplified Bible (AMP)

7 Be still and rest in the Lord; wait for Him and patiently lean yourself upon Him; fret not yourself because of him who prospers in his way, because of the man who brings wicked devices to pass.

Psalm 27:13-14

Amplified Bible (AMP)

13 [What, what would have become of me] had I not believed that I would see the Lord's goodness in the land of the living!

14 Wait and hope for and expect the Lord; be brave and of good courage and let your heart be stout and enduring. Yes, wait for and hope for and expect the Lord.

Isaiah 49:23

Amplified Bible (AMP)

23 And kings shall be your foster fathers and guardians, and their queens your nursing mothers. They shall bow down to you with their faces to the earth and lick up the dust of your feet; and you shall know [with an acquaintance and understanding based on and grounded in personal experience] that I am the Lord; for they shall not be put to shame who wait for, look for, hope for, and expect Me.

Romans 8:24-25

Amplified Bible (AMP)

[24] For in [this] hope we were saved. But hope [the object of], which is seen, is not hope. For how can one hope for what he already sees?

[25] But if we hope for what is still unseen by us, we wait for it with patience and composure.

Isaiah 64:4

King James Version (KJV)

[4] For since the beginning of the world men have not heard, nor perceived by the ear, neither hath the eye seen, O God, beside thee, what he hath prepared for him that waiteth for him.

Isaiah 40:31

Amplified Bible (AMP)

[31] *But those who wait for the Lord [who expect, look for, and hope in Him] shall change and renew their strength and power; they shall lift their wings and mount up [close to God] as eagles [mount up to the sun]; they shall run and not be weary, they shall walk and not faint or become tired.*

Illustration:

Let us now look at one of Jesus' parable on waiting and watchfulness.

Luke 12:35-48

Amplified Bible (AMP)

[35] *Keep your loins girded and your lamps burning,*

[36] *And be like men who are waiting for their master to return home from the marriage feast, so that when he returns from the wedding and comes and knocks, they may open to him immediately.*

37 Blessed (happy, fortunate, and to be envied) are those servants whom the master finds awake and alert and watching when he comes. Truly I say to you, he will gird himself and have them recline at table and will come and serve them!

38 If he comes in the second watch (before midnight) or the third watch (after midnight), and finds them so, blessed (happy, fortunate, and to be envied) are those servants!

39 But of this be assured: if the householder had known at what time the burglar was coming, he would have been awake and alert and watching and would not have permitted his house to be dug through and broken into.

40 You also must be ready, for the Son of Man is coming at an hour and a moment when you do not anticipate it.

41 Peter said, Lord, are You telling this parable for us, or for all alike?

42 And the Lord said, Who then is that faithful steward, the wise man whom his master will set over those in his household service to supply them their allowance of food at the appointed time?

43 Blessed (happy and to be envied) is that servant whom his master finds so doing when he arrives.

44 Truly I tell you, he will set him in charge over all his possessions.

⁴⁵ *But if that servant says in his heart, My master is late in coming, and begins to strike the menservants and the maids and to eat and drink and get drunk,*

⁴⁶ *The master of that servant will come on a day when he does not expect him and at an hour of which he does not know, and will punish him and cut him off and assign his lot with the unfaithful.*

⁴⁷ *And that servant who knew his master's will but did not get ready or act as he would wish him to act shall be beaten with many [lashes].*

⁴⁸ *But he who did not know and did things worthy of a beating shall be beaten with few [lashes]. For everyone to whom much is given, of him shall much be required; and of him to whom men entrust much, they will require and demand all the more.*

So, when I did not receive my expected answers from the Lord, I had to hold onto his promises in the Bible and *'wait for it; because it will surely come.'*

SAFE GUARDS

I need to discuss and advise you of some safe guards for this journey into the spirit world and hearing God's voice.

When I talk about hearing the voice of the Spirit of Almighty God, people sometimes fear that they could get it mixed up with the voice of Satan or the voice of their own heart longings or cravings. They fear if that happened and they acted on it, it could bring real destruction into their lives. Too often, they may think the best solution is not to seek the spiritual life at all, to simply live out of biblical law, and ignore the possibility of hearing from God personally. This is certainly an alternative, and many people have obviously chosen this path, but it is clearly not the way of the abundant life that Jesus promised to us. Instead God has given us several safeguards in scriptures. Then if we will follow them, we can live as Jesus did, comfortable and confident, that we are protected and in the Father's care in both the spiritual and physical worlds.

THE SCRIPTURES

Probably the greatest protection we have on our spiritual journey is the Word of God. A good knowledge of the scriptures can save us from many errors and sorrows. I recommend that those learning to hear God's voice have at least read through the New Testament and Old Testament. This is not to say, of course, that God does not speak to new Christians who have not yet read the word of God. Of course He does! But if they do not couple their prayer time with an intensive study of the word and a relationship with a spiritual counsellor, they can quickly run into danger.

There are two basic ways in which the scriptures can help and protect us.

First, every revelation must be tested against the written word of God. If a revelation violates either the letter of the word or the spirit of the word, it is to be rejected immediately. There is no place for sense or logic, twisting or explaining away the truth of the Bible. There can be no strange, personal interpretations of some unclear verse. The word of the Lord will stand forever and any word to us from God will be in total agreement with both the letter and the spirit of the Eternal Word. We must not only test God's voice in our hearts against the Bible, but also see any revelation as built upon the scriptures. *The Lord told Joshua to meditate upon, confess and act upon the law of God day and night so that He could give him success and prosperity* (**Joshua 1:8**). If I have filled my mind and heart with the Bible, the Holy Spirit will draw forth the precise verses, details or morals I will need in a given situation. The spontaneous flow of illumined scriptures will bring understanding and intuition far greater than my own mind could deliver, if only I will stop briefly and allow myself to be dependent on God.

The **Second** important scriptural safeguard from error and spiritual harm is a humble and teachable spirit (**Isaiah 66:2**). So often the ones who claim to hear from God are arrogant and self-righteous. Their point of view is, 'God told me and that's all there is to it.' *But God resist the proud and gives grace to the humble* (**James 4:6**). Such a proud spirit will eventually cause them to fall into deception. All revelation should be tested (**2 Samuel 22:31**). *Beloved, do not put faith in every spirit, but prove (test) the spirits to discover whether they proceed from God; for many false prophets have gone forth into the world* (**1 John 4:1**). God does not speak to us in order that we may lord it over someone else. Rather, we ought to be known as the meekest of men.

BODY OF CHRIST

We are part of the body of Christ. The full revelation of Jesus does not reside in us individually but only as we come together as a body. I am just a part of the body of Christ. We need to be committed to a local expression of the body of Christ and anyone who wants to venture into the spiritual dimension of life should have a relationship with a spiritual counsellor, whom they respect. They should be accountable. We cannot survive if we try to walk alone. The Lord will show you with whom you are to establish an accountability relationship with if you ask

Him. This is a powerful protection for your life. *In the multitude of counsellors, there is safety* (**Proverbs. 11:14**).

When the Lord revealed these things to me, my immediate decision was to show love. Love is more important than works. Love not productivity, is the centre of the universe. I have begun to slow down and enjoy life, every single minute, and to share this love with the Father and those around me. And if no one is around me, I will just love life and living, and the beauty of His creation. As we have communed together the Lord has made me incredibly productive, even more than I was as a business-man.

Now I enjoy life more, I enjoy my wife, my son, my family, friends, those to whom I minister and those who minister to me. I will never return to being a 'work-a-holic.' Love will always be at the centre of my life.

SUMMARY OF THE FIVE KEYS
Key# 1

I must learn to meet with the Lord regularly in a special place of prayer or to a quiet place, and quieten my own thoughts and emotions, so I could sense the spontaneous flow of God within.

Key# 2

As I pray, I fix the eyes of my heart on Jesus, opening the eyes of my heart to Him, and looking to see what He wanted to show me or speak to me in dreams and visions.

Key# 3

Hearing God's voice is learning what His voice spoken within me would sound like, and God's voice in my heart generally sounds like a flow of spontaneous thoughts. Therefore when I tune to God, I tune to spontaneity.

Key# 4

Journaling, writing out our prayers and God's answers, provides a great new freedom in hearing God's voice. What I learnt from my journaling was there was no need to test it while it was being received, which would stop the flow of God's inner spontaneous thoughts, because I would always have the opportunity later to test and examine it carefully, making sure that it lined up with Scripture.

Key# 5

I must wait for God to bring it to pass; 'It will surely come.' This is the most difficult key to understand because human nature wants answers either now or wants to know when it will happen if it does not happen now. I must understand that, waiting is, by its nature, something only the humble can do with grace.

TESTIMONY

I will end this summary with my testimony showing how putting these five keys together changed my life and brought a financial breakthrough in my family at that time. Becoming still, tuning into spontaneity and to rhema (the spoken word), using vision and journaling brought life into my life and family.

God has been using me in the area of faith, healing, working of miracles and the prophetic for fourteen years. I have seen the dead raised, blind eyes opened all forms of cancer and sickness...etc healed in my ministry but hardly experienced a financial breakthrough.

On the 20th September 2007, my wife delivered our first son into this world by the grace of God here in London, in a foreign land without a pound in our account. I even have to stay without food that day. We had been living not knowing how to pay our rent or feed ourselves on a daily basis from July 2007 which was a period of about six months since my wife lost her job, and I just recently joined her in UK without a job or any other form of support. After seriously meditating on the five keys of hearing God's voice, I got up at midnight, stilled my own thoughts and emotions within me. Suddenly, I heard the Lord saying, "Do you want to know why you are not having breakthrough in your finances?" I positioned myself well and said, "Yes my Lord, I'm longing to know." Then the Lord said, "You have been humble, teachable, obedient to authority and meditating on my word day and night but you are afraid of failure." Then I knew immediately it was true. I surrendered to God, the fear of failure or of being mocked by people, since I knew I had to rely on God alone for my finance. I asked the Lord to show me what to do. Fixing the eyes of my heart on Jesus, "I saw him opening a page, which was very dark. As I kept looking at this page, tiny white lines appeared on the page. These lines are lines of hope" The Lord said, "Don't worry about your finances or what to do. I'm taking care of those tiny white lines you saw on that page myself. Do not ask questions about how it will happen because I'm taking care of you myself. All you need to do is rest on me and by the end of this year, people around you will be thrilled by what I've done in your life and family." I paused to digest this vision when suddenly I saw an angel walk into the room and take my old, torn and crumpled clothes, sat down and ironed them carefully with very straight lines on each of them.

He turned and said to me, "I have made the crooked places straight: I will break in pieces the gates of brass, and cut in sunder the bars of iron. And I will give you the treasures of darkness, and hidden riches of secret places, that you may know I, the Lord which call you by your name, I AM THAT I AM. I will establish you in this town and in time I will make you comfortable. Here you will do what I called you to do, and also for the nations of the world. When I asked you to stop your prosperous business and answer the call for full time ministry in my Kingdom, I made you totally dependent on me financially. Through you I will make many rich, both physical and spiritual, and they will obey Me, to bless you and the work which I called you to do, in whatever way I ask them (**Philippians 4:17; Corinthians 6:10**). Moreover, I'm making you my spokesman," (**Jeremiah 15:19-21**).

I wrote down everything the Lord showed me in my journaling book.
I waited on God, and then about one month later, my wife and I saw a three-bedroom house for rent with a nice garden. At this moment we were living in a one bedroom flat with our son with just fifty pounds left in our bank account. The Lord asked me to give the fifty pounds to a Pastor who was in need and we obeyed. The house rent was £750 and I called the owner and offered £675 by faith. He immediately rejected the offer but invited us to view the property. I went there with my wife and our son's 'UK grandmother.' It was a nice property and we agreed together in prayer and took possession of the property at our price in Jesus name. Two days later I contacted the owner to find out if he had changed his mind, but he told me somebody had already placed the required deposit for the house and he would call me if something went wrong. I thanked the Lord for this possibility of him calling me back ut my wife wailed all night before the Lord. I told my wife that

instead of wailing for the property let us begin to thank God for the financial provision for the house.

The next day the owner of the property called and said, "Why couldn't you let me sleep! What have I done to you! Come and pay me the deposit together with a month's rent tomorrow at your own price." I jumped up and shouted back, 'done'. I was with our son's 'UK grandmother' when he called. Before I could pause and ask questions about where on earth I would get all that money by the next day, our son's 'UK grandmother' told me I have a cheque for your deposit and that she has seen the faithfulness of God in this situation. Later that night, an unexpected source texted me to say that, 'she has a cheque of £6000 for the rent and other needs.' That was more than I could take at that moment.

Two months later, by April 2008, I was comfortably settled in my new home with my family. God has blessed my wife with a new job and is using me to revive the body of Christ.

At the end of 2008, God asked me to start a mission that would set the world on fire for Jesus Christ, to empty hell and populate Heaven and restore the unity of the body of Christ. The name of the mission came into existence through a vision and a Scripture (**Luke 12:49-50**) and has the name World on Fire Mission. Now there is a public ministry of World on Fire mission called The Lord's Vineyard. Find out more about us by visiting our website www.worldonfiremission.org. All Glory is to His name, thanks to my lovely wife, son and my wonderful World on Fire Mission family.

ESTABLISHING AND USING SPIRITUAL ADVISORS

'In the multitudes of counsellors there is safety' (**Proverbs 11:14**)

By God's grace I have three spiritual advisors. In making any major directional moves in my life, a consensus from all my three advisors has been a blessing and I can see God's hand clearly. I always go to them on regular basis to confirm that what I believed I heard from God, actually came from God. The Lord has created me to live in a relationship with and also with one another. It is Satan who seeks to destroy relationships and offers us the spirit of pride which says, 'I know more than you.' Pride is the first sin in the Bible, *'you will be like God knowing good and evil'* (**Genesis 3:5**). *And you said in your heart, I will ascend to heaven; I will exalt my throne above the stars of God; I will sit upon the mount of assembly in the uttermost north. I will ascend above the heights of the clouds; I will make myself like the Most High* (**Isaiah 14:13**).

Pride is the most common sin in the Bible. It is the centre of Satan's heart and I do not want his arrogance in my heart.

God is opposed to the proud, but gives grace to the humble
(**James 4:6**).

1 Thessalonians 5:20-21 exhorts me to *examine everything carefully, hold fast to that which is good; do not despise prophetic utterances.*It is clear from this that there may be errors in the prophetic words I receive (which is essentially what hearing God's voice is) or there would be no need to examine everything carefully and only hold on to the words that are from the Lord.

Suggested Approach to Counselling

We all need counsel from time to time. My wife and I realised that the best counselling in our lives came as we went through our journals, heard God's voice and also received divine counsel for the problems we had faced.

Being counselled by my creator is always the best and the first step for me. When I'm facing problems or seeking God's will for a particular situation or making decisions, after hearing from my Creator, I then seek counsel from a spiritual authority or a mentor. These counsels always comes to me as a confirmation of the counsel I have received from my Creator. A matter is established by the testimony of two or three witnesses (**Deuteronomy 19:15;.John 8:14-18**).

Being healed by the Lord is something I've always practiced when I'm praying, especially when I don't receive answers. Breaking generational sins and ungodly soul ties is very important, especially for someone like me from a royal family in Africa. I come from an upbringing which practices all types of sacrifices offered to idols, the worship of ancestral spirits and evil blood covenants. Breaking the generational sins and ungodly soul ties is very essential in removing negative beliefs and inner vows, and to receive inner healing and deliverance (**Nehemiah 1:6**). It has helped me to learn to walk in the power of the Spirit of life in Christ Jesus, which has brought great healing from the wounds in my heart, through the blood of the Lamb.

So now when people asked me for counsel, I first teach them how to hear God's voice, which will give them a step-by-step coaching so they can clearly hear God's voice in their hearts. It enables a two-way journaling, where they write down what God is saying to them, and their responses back to God. I also ask them to email me two or three journal entries as they get started, so I can encourage and show them that they are on the right path, and truly hearing God's voice. It is always important for people to journal about the problems or decisions they are facing and see what God has to say about it, before seeking counseling. Counseling then comes as a confirmation of what God has already told them and only small directional changes to be made by counselors themselves

CHAPTER 2

DIVINE PATTERNS TO DIALOGUE WITH GOD

The five keys to Hearing God's Voice brought great liberation in my communion with the Lord. Through them, I was able to dialogue with Him most of the time. However, there were still occasions when I couldn't seem to freely communicate with the Lord. I was not able to make spiritual contact and I was confused and could not understand why. I knew I should tune my heart to his voice, but was unable to find the tuning dial! I then discovered that God has laid out for those who seek His direct presence, divine patterns to approach and dialogue with Him.

MOVING FROM LOGOS (LEFT BRAIN ACTIVITY) TO RHEMA (RIGHT BRAIN ACTIVITY

Logos is defined as a tangible or visible form to an idea or quality (letter of the word); an expression of a thought, to collect, to take into account, to relate or appealing to the intellect, to be based on reason or logic and to be spiritual.

Rhema is defined as an indication of that which is spoken (the spirit of the word); that which is expressed in speech or writing, that which is stated intentionally (a declaration, an utterance, an incident, the content or situation).

There is a distinct difference between logos and rhema. Logos is often used to specify the Christian proclamation as the letter of the word, (written word), whereas rhema usually relates to the spirit of the word, (spoken word and utterances).

Jesus declared, "*So Jesus added, when you have lifted up the Son of Man [on the cross], you will realize (know, understand) that I am He [for Whom you look] and that I do nothing of Myself (of My own accord or on My own authority), but I say [exactly] what My Father has taught Me... I tell the things which I have seen and learned at My Father's side, and your actions also reflect what you have heard and learned from your father*" (**John 8:28 & 38**).

When Jesus spoke rhema words, He pricks the heart and touched the emotions of men.
When I speak from the reasoning of my own mind, I may or may not speak to the heart. When I speak the words spoken by His Spirit into my heart and through me, my ministry is more effective.

The question people often asked me is, 'How can I set aside my own reasoning and experience the inner intuitive flow of God?' I want to consider what Elisha did when he needed to hear a prophetic word from God. Elisha knew that to experience the inner intuitive flow of God, he needed to move from logic or reason (left-brain activity) to the word of the Lord spoken intuitively within (flowing through the right side of his brain). Elisha engaged in a right-brain activity, *bring me a minstrel. And while the minstrel played, the hand and power of the Lord came upon [Elisha],* (**2 Kings 3:15**). The music drew him from the left side of his brain to the right side where he was perfectly positioned before the presence of the Lord and able to hear the spontaneous words that were spoken within. The use of vision or enjoying the beauty of nature (both right-brain functions) is able to position me perfectly before the intuitive voice of the Holy Spirit. Speaking in tongues always helps to prepare me more easily to hear the intuitive voice of the Lord.

HOW TO TUNE MY HEART TO HEAR GOD'S VOICE

My mind and physical senses cannot receive the fullness of God's revelation to me. It must come to my heart intuitively through the operation of the Holy Spirit living within me.
"But just as it is written, things which eyes has not seen and ear has not heard, and which have not entered the heart of man, all that God has prepared for those who love Him. For to us God revealed them through the spirit; for the Spirit searches all things, even the depths of God" (**1Corinthians 2:9, 10**).

I learnt that my heart is like a radio, which I need to tune to hear the signals that are coming from God. But what is the tuning device that would help me adjust my heart more perfectly to the voice of God? Now I'm going to show you ways God has said I can tune myself to hear His voice. Most of the aspect of tuning, deals with the preparation of my heart, since it is into the heart that God speaks.

I will look at the **Tabernacle experience** and the instructions given in **Hebrews 10:22.**

APPROACHING GOD THROUGH THE TABERNACLE EXPERIENCE

On Mount Sinai, God gave Moses the design for the Tabernacle where the Israelites were to worship God, offer sacrifices and hear directly from Him. **Hebrews 8:5** tells us that this and the services offered were a copy, a shadow and an example of the heavenly realities. It not only established the way for the Israelites to approach God and hear His voice, but it also demonstrated the way for us.

THE TABERNACLE
The Tabernacle represents the spirit, soul and body of man. **The Outer Courts** correspond to man's body, where we receive knowledge mainly through our five senses. To illustrate this, the outer court did not have a covering but was illuminated by natural light, showing that we receive light, knowledge and revelation, through natural occurrences.

The Holy Place corresponds to man's soul. It had a roof over it, but inside it was illuminated by oil burning in a lamp stand and represented the Holy Spirit, revealing truth to our minds. Oil often symbolizes the Holy Spirit in the Bible.

The Holy of Holies was a totally dark enclosed tent. The only illumination that ever shone inside it was the light of the **Shekinah** glory of God. When God was present there was light. If God departed all was dark. This represented man's spirit, where the glory of God lights our innermost being, giving us direct revelation within our hearts.

There are **six pieces of furniture** in the Tabernacle, which represents the experiences in our approach to God.

In the Outer Court, which represents our body there were two items.

The Brazen Altar, symbolizing the cross (Exodus 27:1-8)
The Brazen (or Bronze) Altar was the first thing you met when you entered the Tabernacle. You could not avoid it. If you wanted to meet with God, you first had to stop at the altar. It was here the priests offered the animal sacrifices to atone for the sins of the people. The Brazen Altar represents my need to make Jesus the Lord of my life and present myself as a living sacrifice to Him (**Romans 12:1-2**). It represents the cross directly inside the gate of salvation. Just as he offered Himself

as a sacrifice for me, Jesus now asks me to offer myself for Him. Paul said, *I have been crucified with Christ* (**Galatians 2:20**).

I am often tempted to shy away from the Brazen Altar. I want to avoid it if at all possible because it is hot. It means death to my flesh, laying down what I want and desiring only His will. I must do it daily. I cannot go around it. This is where my first spiritual sense is activated, the eyes of my heart.

The Brazen Laver, representing God's word (Exodus 30:17-21)

The Brazen (or Bronze) Laver was a large basin where the Priests washed their hands and feet before moving into the Holy Place. It had two layers for hands and feet. If they entered into the Holy Place without stopping here to cleanse themselves they would die. In **Ephesians 5:26-27**, Paul spoke of how Jesus cleansed and sanctified us by the washing of water with the word. So also the Laver signified the washing of me by applying the Logos (Word of God, Scripture) to my life. The applied Logos has a cleansing effect on my heart and mind. I do not need any special revelation to understand and obey God's commandment. It is interesting that the Brazen Laver was made from mirrors that the Hebrew women donated for the building of the Tabernacle. In **James 1:22-24**, those who read the word but do not obey it are compared with someone who looks in a mirror and sees that his face is dirty and his hair untidy but does nothing to fix himself up and just walks away without making any changes. As I read the Bible, God holds up a mirror to my heart showing what I really look like. As I approach God, He wants me to be changed, sanctified and made holy by applying the cleansing power of His word to my life daily. It is here that my second spiritual sense is activated, the ears of my heart.

After stopping by the Brazen Laver to be washed, the Priest then moved to the holy place, which was a large room with a roof of animal skins.

Inside the holy place, there are three pieces of furniture.
The Table of Showbread, symbolizing our will (Exodus 25:23-30)
This was the table where the priests placed 12 special loaves of bread. Just as flour is ground fine for the making of the bread, so my will is ground fine as I totally commit my ways to the Lord. God wants my will to be set only to obey Him, when I enter His presence and to hear from Him.
The Priests come together to eat this bread on a weekly basis. God uses my fellowship with other believers as a means of grinding my will and shaping me into his image. It is here that my third spiritual sense is activated, the will of my heart.

The Golden Lamp Stand, representing our illumined mind (Exod. 25:31-39)

Inside the holy place there was a Golden Lamp Stand containing seven oil lamps. This gave light to the holy place. The oil represents the Holy Spirit. The seven oil lamps represent the seven Spirits of the Lord; the Spirit of the Lord, the Spirit of wisdom, the Spirit of understanding, the Spirit of counsel, the Spirit of might, the Spirit of knowledge and the Spirit of the fear of the Lord (**Isaiah 11:2**). God enlightens my mind with His revelation and His truth, when I meditate on His word and do my journaling. The book of Luke was written in this way. Luke stated, "*In as much as many have undertaken to compile an account of the things accomplished among us .... it seemed fitting for me as well, having investigated everything carefully from the beginning, to write it out for you in consecutive order ...... so that you might know the exact truth about the things you have been taught*" (**Luke 1:1-4**). In other words, Luke carefully studied everything he could find about Jesus, analysed it and organised it, under the illumination of the Holy Spirit and wrote down the result of his work.

I often prepare my sermons this way. He breathes into my mind His wisdom and knowledge and I have learned to allow intuition and spontaneity to flow into my reasoning processes thereby allowing my heart and mind to work together, like the seven-branched Lamp Stand. It is here that my fourth spiritual sense is activated, the mind of my heart.

The Altar of Incense, representing our Emotions (Exodus 30:1-10)

Immediately in front of the doorway to the Holy of Holies, was a golden table where the priest burned an offering of incense every morning and evening. This table was perfectly square and balanced. The incense represents the praise of God's people. The way into the Holy of Holies, the manifest presence of God, is through praise and worship. As I offer up a continuous sacrifice of praise, my emotions are brought under the control of the Holy Spirit and come into perfect balance. God is enthroned on the praises of His people (**Psalm 22:3**).

The all-square aspect of the altar indicates an emotional life that is perfectly balanced. An emotional balance is difficult in view of the pressures of life. I can often swing from optimism to pessimism, from faith to fear and from joy to despair. There is really only one way my emotional life can be brought to a balance point and remain there. That way is Jesus, and my approach to Him is through worship, praise and thanksgiving. In **1Thessalonians 5:18**, Paul told us to give thanks in everything. In every situation God is worthy of my praise. And through the continuous offering of a sacrifice of praise, my emotions can be brought under the control of the Holy Spirit. Only He can bring me into this perfect balance. The psalmist declares that we should *enter God's gates with thanksgiving and His court with praise* (**Psalm 100:4**).

The Horns of the altar were the highest point of the holy place and were the same height as the furniture in the Holy of Holies. Worship lifts me to this level and moves me into the Holy of Holies, which represents man's spirit. Praise and worship are the best ways to quiet my heart and touch Christ within me. It is here that my fifth and last spiritual sense is activated, the emotions of my heart.

Inside the holy place, was a smaller, separate room called the **Holy of Holies.** Inside this 'tent of meeting' was just one item.

The Ark symbolizes Direct Revelation of the Spirit into our Hearts (Exod. 25: 10-22).

The Holy of Holies represents our spirits, where we can have direct communion with the Lord. In the old covenant, only the High Priest was permitted to go through the veil, and only once a year on the Day of Atonement. When Jesus died on the cross, the veil separating us from God's direct presence was torn from top to bottom, opening the way for me to have moment-by-moment fellowship with Almighty God.

The Ark of Covenant was a chest made of acacia wood overlaid with pure gold. In it was placed the tablets on which the Ten Commandments were written, Aaron's rod that had budded and a jar of manna (**Hebrews 9:4**). The cover of the Ark was called the mercy seat, over it were two Cherubim fashioned of pure gold facing each other, their wings spread upward to cover the mercy seat. It was from **the mercy seat** that God promised to meet with and speak to Moses and the priests. This reminds me that out of worship and stillness, I enter into heart-to-heart communion with God, as His glory fills my spirit. It is in the quietness of my heart that I hear God speak to me.

The manna in the Ark reminds me of God's supernatural provision. As I wait in the presence of the Lord, receiving direct revelation from Him within my spirit, supernatural life and strength flow up from deep within me. This strengthens me to face the trials of life in victory and His divine life flowing through me and out of me meets the need of a hurting world. **Aaron's rod** that budded was a divine affirmation of the God-given authority. God's word gives me authority (**Luke 10:19**). When I meet face-to-face with my Father as Moses did, and hear His Spirit speak to my spirit, and I speak what I have heard from God, my words come forth with divine authority, (**2 Corinthians 3:12**).

The Ten Commandments represents the Law of God, the standard of holiness required to meet with Him. When I come to God, I come to perfect holiness. But remember what has been placed above the Law; the mercy seat. Jesus Christ has made atonement for my sins. Through His blood I am cleansed and made pure so I can have fellowship with the Holy One. I receive access to boldly come to the throne of grace.

I do not follow the procedure of the Tabernacle every time I pray. I always try to live my life in line with the requirements represented by each piece of furniture. But when I have trouble hearing from the Lord, when my prayers seems to be bounce off the ceiling and echo in the room, I come to the Tabernacle to find out why. I do this by seeing myself before each piece of furniture and asking the Lord to speak to me through it. I usually find the reason for the breakdown in communication by the time I enter the Holy of Holies. By this wonderful tool, I am able to tune my heart once again to hear what the Lord wants to say to me.

The Tabernacle is a means to help me see the condition of my heart. I use it to accomplish my goal, which is to live in a day-to-day, moment-by-moment fellowship with our Lord and Saviour, Jesus Christ.

B) HEBREWS 10:19-22; PRESENTS A WONDERFUL APPROACH FOR HEARING GOD'S VOICE

Discovering the place of the Tabernacle experience in my prayer life enables me to tune my heart to hear the Lord much more consistently, and through it, I could usually discover the reason for any inability I had to break through to dialogue with God. Still, occasionally I present myself before each piece of furniture, asking Jesus to reveal any failure to live according to the principle represented by it. I then found myself going all the way into the Holy of Holies without being convicted, yet unable to enter into dialogue and fellowship with the Father.

Hebrews 10:19-22
New King James Version (NKJV)
19 Therefore, brethren, having boldness to enter the Holiest by the blood of Jesus, 20 by a new and living way which He consecrated for us, through the veil, that is, His flesh, 21 and having a High Priest over the house of God, 22 let us draw near with a true heart in full assurance of faith, having our hearts sprinkled from an evil conscience and our bodies washed with pure water.

I see here, the honours and benefits, which our Lord Jesus Christ has obtained for me. The benefits are, *having boldness to enter the Holiest* (v. 19). I am now rightfully admitted into God's presence to receive direction, and also have the freedom of spirit and speech to abide by the direction. I have the right to enter into communion with God. I understand that fallen man cannot abide with God without a high priest, who is the mediator of reconciliation (**Hebrews 8:6**) here on earth. But accepting Jesus Christ into my life, who is *a high priest over the house of God* (v. 21), gives me the boldness to abide with God.

We see the means by which I enjoy such benefits, declared to me *by the blood of Jesus* (v. 19). This boldness to approach God is a result of the blood of Jesus, which He offered up to God as an atoning sacrifice for me. This blood being, sprinkled on my conscience, drives away fear and doubt, and gives me confidence both for my safety and freedom into His divine presence.

Having the full account of the way in which we have access to God, I now know it is the only way (**1 Timothy 2:5**) to the tree of life since the way to the first tree of life has been closed (**Genesis 3:22-24**). It is *a new way* (v. 20), not a result of my works, so that I may not boast or consider it my own doing; it is the gift of God, by grace through my faith in our Lord and Saviour, Jesus Christ (**Ephesians 2:8-9**). This is the last and only way that will ever be open to men for salvation (**Acts 4:12**). Those who will not enter through this way will keep themselves out forever. It is a way that will always be sufficient. It is *a living way* (v. 20). It would be death if I come to God by my works and my sinful nature; but by this living way, we come to God, and we will live (**Romans 8:6-9**). It is by this living Saviour, who, although was dead, is alive, and gives me life, hope and a future. It is *by a new and living way, which He consecrated for us, through the veil, that is, His flesh* (v. 20). The veil in the tabernacle represents the body of Christ; and when he died, the veil of the temple was torn in two (**Luke 23:44-45**), and this was at the time of the evening sacrifice.

This gave the people a surprising view into the holy of holies, which they never seen before. Our only way to heaven is by a crucified Saviour. His death gave me life and also to those who will believe in Him (**John 3:16**).

Verse 22 showed me how to draw near to God, and the right manner to come into God's presence. I must draw near to God in humble adoration and with a heart of worship. I must make my approach to God with a right altitude as follows;

1) With a True Heart.

My heart must be true, without any craftiness or hypocrisy. With no deception and no lying. I know that, the Spirit of God searches everything and He requires truth in my heart (**1 Corinthians 2:10-11**). *For the eyes of the* LORD *run to and fro throughout the whole earth, to show Himself strong on behalf of those whose heart is loyal to Him* (**2 Chronicles 16:9**). I am wholehearted in my love, praise and trust of God. I return to Him with my whole heart; I search for Him with my whole heart; and I cry out to Him with my whole heart.

2) In Full Assurance of Faith.

With my faith developed to a full confidence, urging me that when I come to God, I know that I will have communion with Him, and be accepted by Him. I also know that without faith, it is impossible to please God (**Hebrews 11:6**). I have come to a decision to believe all that God says about me is true. I have an unshakable conviction that God lives in my heart and that His river flows out from within me. *For if what is passing away was glorious, what remains is much more glorious. Therefore, since we have such hope, we use great boldness of speech* (**2 Corinthians 3:11-12**) to come into his presence with full assurance of faith. When I come before God with a receptive heart to His inner river, the resulting flow is God. My God is *Immanuel, which is translated, God with us* (**Matthew 1:23**). All doubt and unbelief is defeated. I am a believer (**Mark 11:22-24**).

3) Having my Heart Sprinkled from An Evil Conscience.

I need to have my heart sprinkled from an evil conscience by applying the blood of Jesus to my soul by faith in Him. I absolutely believe that as I confess my sins before God, they are totally washed away by the blood of Jesus. I am cleansed from guilt, corruption, fear and torment. *There is no fear in love; but perfect love casts out fear, because fear involves torment. But he who fears has not been made perfect in love* (**1 John 4:18**). I have been made perfect in the love of Christ. I stand clean and holy before God, not because of my righteousness, but because of the cleansing blood of Christ.

This is what makes me righteous before God. It is not I; it is through Christ.

4) My Body Washed with Pure Water.

My body is washed with pure water by the word of God. I am washed pure by His word to endow me with the morals of holiness and be cleansed from guilt, contamination and being controlled by sin. *Christ also loved the church and gave Himself for her,* [26] *that He might sanctify and cleanse her with the washing of water by the word* (**Ephesians 5:25-26**). When God speaks to me in prayer, I must allow it to cleanse me by applying and abiding in his word. I have often found in my own life that God has nothing to say to me if I have not obeyed the last word He gave me. His grace may allow me to continue in communication for a time, but there comes a point when I must either obey or relinquish my communion with God. *To obey is better than sacrifice* (**1 Samuel 15:22**). God is not interested in how many hours I spend with Him if I only hear and do not obey.

Since discovering and applying this passage to my prayer life, not a single day has gone by that I have been unable to make Spirit-to-Spirit contact with the Lord.

CHAPTER 3

CONCLUSION

Staying in God's Presence

I must stay in God's presence all day long, receiving revelation continuously as I walk through my daily life. This is the way Jesus lived;

So Jesus answered them by saying, I assure you, most solemnly I tell you, the Son is able to do nothing of Himself (of His own accord); but He is able to do only what He sees the Father doing, for whatever the Father does is what the Son does in the same way [in His turn].

The Father dearly loves the Son and discloses to (shows) Him everything that He Himself does. And He will disclose to Him (let Him see) greater things yet than these, so that you may marvel and be full of wonder and astonishment.

*I am able to do nothing from myself [independently, of my own accord—but only as I am taught by God and as I get His orders]. Even as I hear, I judge [I decide as I am bidden to decide. As the voice comes to me, so I give a decision], and my judgment is right (just, righteous), because I do not seek or consult my own will [I have no desire to do what is pleasing to myself, my own aim, my own purpose] but only the will and pleasure of the Father Who sent Me. (**John 5:19, 20& 30**).*

This is how I am to live. I do not fall in and out of His presence. I stay in His presence by maintaining the biblical posture, which is described above. The Bible calls it, 'Abiding in Christ' (**John 15:7**) and *'Pray without Ceasing'* (**1 Thessalonians 5:17**). I can now say like Paul, *'I have strength for all things in Christ who empowers me [I am ready for anything and equal to anything through Him who infuses inner strength into me; I am self-sufficient in Christ's sufficiency],'* (**Philippians 4:13**).

I will now conclude what God has taught me. How God has asked me to change my life, and how I'm influencing other lives using the five keys of hearing God's voice, by quoting the words of Paul on his trip to the church in Corinth A.D. 51;

1 Corinthians 2:1-5

As for myself, brethren, when I came to you, I did not come proclaiming to you the testimony and evidence or mystery and secret of God [concerning what He has done through Christ for the salvation of men] in lofty words of eloquence or human philosophy and wisdom (v. 1).

Paul showed me here the manner in which we should preach the good news of our Lord Jesus Christ. Paul's preaching was not with captivating and persuasive words of human philosophy and wisdom. But he came among them proclaiming the testimony of our Lord Jesus Christ for the salvation of men. He declared a divine revelation and gave adequate facts for the authority of the revelation, both by its agreement to ancient predictions and by its present miraculous operations. I learnt here that lofty words of eloquence or human philosophy and wisdom would add no weight to the authority of the Spirit of God.

For I resolved to know nothing (to be acquainted with nothing, to make a display of the knowledge of nothing, and to be conscious of nothing) among you except Jesus Christ (the Messiah) and Him crucified (v. 2).

Paul was determined to know no other knowledge than this, to preach nothing and to discover the knowledge of nothing and to be conscious of nothing, but Jesus Christ, and Him crucified. He understood that Christ, in His person and offices, is the sum and substance of the gospel. Christ and Him crucified should be at the heart and centre of my preaching. My mission is to proclaim the gospel of the cross and invite people under the banner of the cross for the salvation of their souls. *But far be it from me to glory [in anything or anyone] except in the cross of our Lord Jesus Christ (the Messiah) through whom the world has been crucified to me, and I to the world* (**Galatians 6:14**).

And I was in (passed into a state of) weakness and fear (dread) and great trembling [after I had come] among you (v. 3).

Maybe Paul had a small stature, a low voice with no eloquence of speech as his enemies in the church of Corinth spoke of him. *'For his letters,' they say, 'are weighty and powerful, but his bodily presence is weak, and his speech contemptible'* (**2 Corinthians 10:10**). But although he had no eloquence of speech as some say, it is clear from scripture that he was not an inferior speaker. *Now when the people saw what Paul had done, they raised their voices, saying in the Lycaonian language, 'The gods have come down to us in the likeness of men.' And Barnabas they called Zeus, and Paul, Hermes, because he was the chief speaker* (**Acts 14:11-12**). Paul acted in his office with much humility, unpretentiousness, reserve and care. He behaved in great trembling among them as one reserved to approve himself faithful, not having sufficiency in himself, in order not to misrepresent his office. Paul in his own words says, *but I discipline my body and bring it into subjection, lest, when I have preached to others, I myself should become disqualified* (**1 Corinthians 9:27**). The Lord says, *'But on this one will I look: On him who is poor and of a contrite spirit, and who trembles at My word,'* (**Isaiah 66:2**). King David says, *'the sacrifices of God are a broken spirit, a broken and a contrite heart— These, O God, You will not despise,'* (**Psalm 51:17**). My life was completely touched and changed by this nature, which is emphasised in Christ.

And my language and my message were not set forth in persuasive (enticing and plausible) words of wisdom, but they were in demonstration of the [Holy] Spirit and power [a proof by the Spirit and power of God, operating on me and stirring in the minds of my hearers the most holy emotions and thus persuading them], (v. 4).

Paul's language and message was not given by enticing and plausible words of a wise philosopher, or by winning the peoples' minds to himself by a display of words. He did not show a pompous demonstration of wise reasoning and extraordinary skills. He did not set himself to please and entertain the desires of the people with lofty words of eloquence or human philosophy and wisdom. But they were in demonstration of the Holy Spirit, and of the power of God. *For the kingdom of God does not consist in talk but in power* (**1 Corinthians 4:20**). He spoke as the Spirit gave him utterance to deliver the Good News of the gospel of Jesus Christ while the Lord was working with him in confirming the Word by the attesting signs *and* miracles that closely accompanied it (**Mark 16:20**). This is how I learnt to serve God. Amen

So that your faith might not rest in the wisdom of men (human philosophy), but in the power of God (v. 5).

Paul ended here with his mission statement. He preached Christ crucified in this manner, so that they might not be carried by human philosophy and motives, or overcome by simple human arguments and quarrels. It should not be said that either eloquence or logic resulted in them becoming Christians. But when nothing but Christ crucified was plainly preached, the favourable outcome was founded not on human philosophy, but by divine evidence and impact. The gospel was preached in such a way that God was at the heart and centre of it, and was to be glorified in everything.

This is now my mission to set the world on fire and why Christ crucified is at the heart and centre of everything and He is to be glorified in all. Amen. *Thus says the Lord: Let not the wise and skilful person glory and boast in his wisdom and skill; let not the mighty and powerful person glory and boast in his strength and power; let not the person who is rich [in physical gratification and earthly wealth] glory and boast in his [temporal satisfactions and earthly] riches; But let him who glories glory in this: that he understands and knows Me [personally and practically, directly discerning and recognizing My character], that I am the Lord, Who practices loving-kindness, judgment, and righteousness in the earth, for in these things I delight, says the Lord* (**Jeremiah 9:23-24**)